GLASS FACTORY

Also by Marilyn McCabe:

Perpetual Motion

GLASS FACTORY

Marilyn McCabe

THE WORD WORKS
WASHINGTON, D.C.

THE WORD WORKS
P.O. Box 42164
Washington, D.C. 20015
editor@wordworksbooks.org

Cover design: Susan Pearce Design
Cover art: *Up and Down* (detail) by Victoria Palermo, 2015,
a site-specific installation commissioned
by the Albany International Airport, Albany, NY.
Photo courtesy of Arthur Evans.
Author photograph: Kathleen McGee

LCCN: 2015959362
ISBN: 978-1-944585-05-1

Acknowledgments

Poems have also been published in the following journals:

The Bitter Oleander: "Incarnate"
Cellpoems: "Forgetting"
The Literary Review: "The East Field" and "The Details"
Los Angeles Review: "On Hearing the Call to Prayer over the Marcellus Shale on Easter Morning," winner AROHO Orlando Prize
Pine Hills Review: "Cape May"
Right Hand Pointing: "Two Crows" and "Mercy: Bird in Hand"
Solstice Literary Magazine: "This liquid in state of frozen chaos holds" and "I await the night with dread; await the night with longing"
Valparaiso Poetry Review: "Lakeshore Limited"

"The Curve Traced Out from a Point That Moves So Its Distance from the Point Is Constant" (in a slightly different form) and "River II" appeared in the anthology *The Lake Rises* (Stockport Flats, 2013).

"Lilly, PA" appeared in *Van Gogh's Ear Anthology* (2012).

CONTENTS

I AWAIT THE NIGHT WITH DREAD; AWAIT THE NIGHT WITH LONGING

With its black strokes, singing,
it smears me, lavish.

I'm the night's white canvas,
                          turbulent and stiff.

I can grab the burning
stars in my hand.

But I can't let them loose.

THE DARK IS SHIFTING ALMOST IMPERCEPTIBLY

toward you. I know that much
of endings. As usual I'm mistaken,
though, about what's moving.

Not the dark onward but you
and I falling toward it, and sometimes
it is beautiful, framed in flame,

and some days, as today, obscure.
Hymn will lead you
humming. I hope.

STONE CHURCH ROAD

Sometimes lying hours awake I can almost hear
the deer sweep through the undergrowth,
ring the house, its small barn,

past the apple trees, gnarled and spent.
I leave the lights off
and sometimes float from the room,

discover a silence that expands
to fill the night, push back the walls,
the skylight; field with the deer whose breath

twines up the trunks of white pine that, voiceless
in a slight wind, tower somber, dimmer
than clouds. They deepen in the damp

soil, roots spreading just below
the surface, unreliable, shallow,
where burrow the beetles, their subtle

snap, and ants in a rush
turn the mulch and duff, the loam
that gathers them all here.

I admit I am afraid
of this departure of space into
slow dripping time until I am aware

only of my own breathing, the heaviness of my tongue.
I want to sing to the deer,
to stop their furtive departure,

usher them inside — their large eyes,
enormous noses, the smooth flanks
where muscle resides, the small twitches.

I stay motionless at the window.
I can't really see them at all,
only the absence of pine against

star spattered sky, the vague
recollection of light.
If there are deer

they are lost to me. What I thought
I heard only the hum of refrigerator,
scratch of mice, drum of pulse.

SELF-SIGHT

The body's a thing and such,
decommissioned, a vessel:
pipes and containers that left
to their own devices will desiccate,
crumble. I fainted at the first
cut and so missed the rest,
escorted out before the buzz

saw hit the skull. But was I
surprised at the body so
unsound? Or did I identify
too closely with the corpse; ironic,
as what is human of me is least
corporeal: mood, memory, and that other
impulse: the soul's
determination not to be alone.

Goldsworthy Variations

1. On Maintaining Optimism

A rawness, wrenching strength of roots,
their wanton destruction, the mending ways of mud,
the merging power of minerals under weight, scattered,
mindless search of flood, but a yielding too
of softened fibers, bark to moss; sometimes
we surprise each other, the way terrain is revealed
in the slow nudity of November, and we see
each other's landscapes, hear another's
rivulet and road, the sudden tumble of snow from bough.

2. Continuum

The last work I make will be a hole, the black
hole of my pruned energy, raisined reason,
icy with my inner fires. And so we are buried
in what we came from, though in life we've mistaken
dark for death, light for something to strive for.
Gravity, though physicists may quibble, I imagine,
makes us endless, and what I think is a frisson of your ghost
may be the wormhole of you coming home.

3. What nature tosses, man *must* assemble,

or dismember, modify, render,
yet we can be tender
makers, one stone atop another,
massage of mud and wheat
baked in heat, scratched, tapped,
set next to what we also consider beauty:
swell of hill, etch of birch forest
along the lengthy study of old sea
and glacier, the scattered river's
arrest, until some days all
we see is the coming together of chaos
to order and its lovely drifting apart.

Mercy: Bird in Hand

I've folded for you five paper cranes,

one breeze, a harness,

tied these strings

with which the cranes will carry

you, feather and bone.

THE IDEA OF ANTARCTICA

Poised on the axis *i*:
ice exclamation point,
to Earth's surprise,
and fire too, as two
poles are never far apart.
Some center of gravitas
and silence, time-
less, light,
dark, and the bruits of a breathing
thing, its tics, sighs. No end
in sight.

* * *

Step into white
Your step
is white
Foot white In seconds you
are white If it is night
white white day
Step two three already
there is no
back is white
no forward
Wind white
White hand is no
hand You are tied to
white others
If one goes down
white white

* * *

Where does the world end?

Where do I begin?

Negative space

against skin

a dotted line,

its many mouths

often confused.

Pointilist and wide

open, you can see

right through me,

almost. Everywhere

the easing of out-

lines until what was

gone is gone and here

in curve, half

seen: what is

revealed in absence.

HOMEAWAY

Even her home has become alien,
plates and cups wander around,
what yesterday's hand did today's has forgotten.

Her own writing appears mysteriously.
Plants no longer bloom,
nor live in their pots no longer on the sill.

A familiar flower has no name,
nor that bird that makes no song.
Butter has appeared in some strange dish.

She is becoming brocade and breeze
in socks, her little pointed toes.
What's forgotten's forgotten but these lines:

the frost is on the pumpkin,
the goldenrod green,

half a league,
half a league,
half a league dilly dilly,
and I will be queen.

THE DOMINION OF LIGHT, MAGRITTE

Day and night are everywhere
light in your mansion mind.
Whirl away in the crepuscular cup
the exquisite hour of opposites.

The light is undoing the dying;
the dying dismantling this life.
You can slip out behind the trees.
Get while the going is good.

Lakeshore Limited

Skeletal small towns' rebar remains,
heart of a grange hall, a church revealed, shards
pierce and work their way inwards, shattered
bones all alight. A coil of brown barbed

wire, a torqued stave, some fence rod or road tie,
the curled hand of a man blasted
by sun, rain, snow hip deep. How we unfold
across our own horizon, beautiful

waste of our made things strew,
slow destruction of our mettle.

Night Sky

Orion leapt through my window last night,

        hard edges, sharp angles.
He pressed me to him and I felt the bite

of the stars of his belt against my ribs.

                His kiss was all darkness.

I slid into the space between stars and disappeared.

But the sharp dark was revealed at last
            to be curves and sweet tastes.
        And I slept in his pale embrace
under the shroud of moon

so light. I did not feel him slip away.

Remember me

On Pina Bausch's "Café Müller"

Falling clatter

chairs, the bodies.

The void behind. I drop
forward, drown.

Grasp to lose,
I fall from you.

Light ground as a lens,
to see, to see such small: o self

strained   to build   to push:
(Am I these walls?)

Home.
Home.
I do not know where to go.

But, ah,

forget my fate.

CAPE MAY

Brave son of wind and wire we are
lust and foolish Capable of touch and tender
bleeding All wave weave Barely blue
sky admires our bigness Wind our capacity
individually for quiet Tall grass wheat and white wanders
                                                            down a cleft
to divide to lose to rock the sand sea kelp tangle urchin
flesh Hides and is revealed tonight the clouds
race a breeze of stars between their lacing arms falling falling.

Planting

The last cherry of early summer is in the white bowl,
portly, marooned in a slight pool of its own juice
seeping from a small wound. The end
sometimes seems sweeter than we'd imagined,
and more tart even than we'd feared.

When we plant the pit still stained
in salt-damped soil, we are sure we can conjure
some abundance for the empty bowl,
to imagine, in absence, something
that will branch. Bloom.

Via Flaminia

for Kay

We crush thyme under our feet
and it rises, as if we are

robed in it, this month of Julius,
heavy, blue. Stones disappear

down the hill into thicket
again as we climb and stumble

along the flaming way,
now worn and grown over,

a song of meats, tomato.
The chapel's light is milk

through the alabaster,
drunk with old texts, but

the buzzing touch of fallen
plums is a new word.

Incarnate

A beak and one quarter of a skull.
Small something: song bird, sparrow,

the left behind of a short life, the rest
shattered and sifted already by a flick of soil

feeding the holes where, tender pressed,
the carrot seeds will peck downward, their oriole

glow buried; but one plume will wing skyward,
as I am gorgeous with my dead, and full of mysteries.

DERMIS

The skin's a beast,
boils and blooms,
it may brag
or moan the slow road down,
incessant fold.
Layered, it sheds, unthreads as a rag.
It can't be killed with an ordinary wound.
First it clings. Then it swoons.

* * *

My edges stratify. I transform
to something yielding
as a shadow in the hands of late afternoon.

* * *

Vast organ, you expand
to meet the edges of my coarse cathedral,
the clustered hungers of its congregate.

* * *

See how this twisted floss
of voices embroiders you,
my weary shroud.

* * *

Sticks and stones break my bones.
The earth is littered with me.
Skin in silence moans.
It's time that tells/untells me.

* * *

Fossiled, I am impressed,
hollowed but ornate. World
on skin eats at me;
the encounter,
wearing away in memory,
leaves strange shapes and spaces.

"MARCELLE"

What it's come to: a hand, just one,
long fingers like his mother's,
wide nails clipped short,
the reach, the grasp, one
syllable, no, two: enough
to say his brother's name.

A searching eye, just one,
face to face to sand to
the water. Say water.
We are on the edge.
It is too much to say this.
The skin of the hand
is so smooth.

Munch's *Melancholy*

The ship has never come and waiting
has weakened the seascape to languid,
a drunken tide, even the stones
falter to sand in the waiting. Half
sea, the horizon, half the blocky

forms of man's hand,
his fortresses and barns,
his nervous harness of everything
that seems uncontrollable.
But the man himself is clear; waiting

has made him firmer, has rouged his cheek.
He appears to sleep but is dreaming, is
awake to how sea and sky —
as waiting, as living —
are two parts of the same thing.

The Details

From my mother I learned to value the bird,
haphazard flock of robins, the fine-penned jay,

the downy woodpecker upside down
on the butternut; and this: tufted criss-cross of contrail

across a sky. My teen self eye-rolling at her,
endlessly agape, but now I find

my eye is still on the x,
that I too never tire of looking.

That this may save me from myself,
savage, of the woods. I know little of prayer but this

watching: a cedar waxwing, its extravagant markings,
its clever beak that does not pierce,

that does not pierce
the berry's skin.

Long Haul

At night sometimes I hear

     less a sound than some chug of thump
and I wonder if a dog has strayed into my home

          to scratch at fleas or a sleepwalking
construction worker is shifting dirt with a backhoe

then realize   it's a train on the far tracks
carrying freight through the night

and I think radioactive waste or flammable oil and the
conductor, sleepy,
     connects the dots of light with an uneasy pulse,

like commerce needs to watch its weight, its EKG erratic;

     awake now I forget how to breathe and
the train becomes my own

beating arteries, heart driving its cargo across my body,
       a shipment that might itself ignite.

FACTORY RUIN

Bagged and billowing,
mooching groundward,
tatter of atoms giving up.
Time not so much healer as

the peeling label torn of its shelf life,
hole maker, letting in light,
wet, wind. It will end
in unguent.

Even the stiffest
metals deliquesce.
And we, re-primitivized, re-wild,
the last of us licking what's left.

The East Field

The east field is a giant's cheek,
bedrock so close to the surface here.

It turns out that water is not the only mutable
element, from sea to cloud to downpour; rock too

has its cycle: igneous may crystallize
to the wink of quartz,

weather and wear to weepy sediment,
then be pressed to metamorph,

so I must conclude flesh and bone
also know the way of change

and seem to manifest today
as small ghosts studding the damp grass.

But look, as through a curtain, the field appears
worn as an old horse's teeth

from chewing the wind that blows now
the pale rain sideways.

THIS LIQUID IN STATE OF FROZEN CHAOS HOLDS

my forehead. I lean against it, regard the snow
that would not hold me, its agreements
more lax, more wink and nudge.

Your skin feels firm beneath my hand,
though time's already taxed its elasticity
around your edges, and the thought that this too,

warm solid, will someday liquefy
terrifies. In the morning I go out onto the lake.
The fishermen and I rely on the tacit consonance of ice:

That it will not yield. Will not crack.
Though we appear to walk on black
sky, its milky constellations.

Prague

The river, frosted and charmed, takes,
in its turbulence, in its ripple and shoals,

city, castle and stone, bridge by bridge,
and red roofs, hills, foot-smoothed roads.

Takes the square where saints ring round the hour, seven
synagogues, the circle of dead. It unclenches

my fingers from around the reeds
and quenches my stinking fires. The eyes

on the Charles Bridge turn inward;
grime wraps them in velvet over the river. The river

has lipped across the cobbles, its syllables
hard fallen, consonants tortured. There is a gate.

A man in a window. A window. I
wear my crown and a worn overcoat of thin woven wool.

It seems I've been a stranger.
The river does not know my name.

Two Crows

Absence in trees. Slash. Slash.
This is how the abyss is winged.
Lord, let me not get close enough
to see their awful eyes.

Forgetting

Clouds misremember
sky sometimes. Ice preserves
what it can of ocean.

THE FACE OF THE WATERS

What moves on the face of waters
but the wind, shifting sky, the restless
eyes of clouds?

Water thirsts at island's edge.
Canoes thump in
fitful sleep.

The bear came again last night,
and again, dragging away
our vat of dreams

to the beach, to
the lake's restive face
and steady laugh.

In the morning I put my hand
in the print of the beast's sole, stare
to the dim horizon:

Again there is earth; heaven. Water
in between. We break camp.
It's a long row home

in God's teeth,
his snuffling nostrils.
Scent of musk, damp duckweed.

December, Pitchoff Mountain

Whirled the eye takes the wind gone wild with it

Across the frozen wetland shattering a cliff face into shards

Submerged one mitten now mosaic now emerged

Sorry we are to hurtle through here and therefore grab
what we think stills us

Another's hand another eye that in the incessant motion
of this ride seems solid

But we flail the landscape flies around us

Until our parts are obscured and the eye gone sky

River

Fingers in every crevice.
Carry with me trunks and cloaks.
Taken walls. Some hours I blithely destroy.
Wrenched handrail, a hat sodden, blue wool, stolen sneakers.

I am not responsible.

Driven by furrow, frenzy, the far clouds,
untied and mud soiled. Dammed
here. There straying, fringed, forgetting.
Deepening, I depend on the cycle
of my own disintegration.

Hardangervidda Plateau, Norway

white swan

white river

linen light

starched tight

woven winter

the first season

time a fissure

salted

tidal

rose hips

dark as old blood

where wind has been

is bitten sheared pocked

and the wind

it has been everywhere

Lilly, PA

The layered deaths of small things
made black the heart of these hills,
and the streams, washed gullies, the great river
carry the dead's murmur
to roar, drowned now
by the chunk chunk of machine,
rake and clang of cargo cars,
the squeak as they pull away,
rust-feathered, driven.

Shadows come early in the hollows,
ice lies late. The crooked railroad
ties them all here
in the wrinkled palm of this off-god's hand.
Fathers wasted want on lack,
the fabric of cheesecloth
brought home to the women for cranberries,
bought in half-yards from bolts
at the dusty back of the 5&10
with coins from pockets
lined with the lint of the realm, rich
with reinforced seams, Wrangler rivets,
the yellow w's of their leaving.

The war was a gift:
young men, fresh-shaved and willing
to tie honor on like a wool scarf,
wear it to the field,
my father to sea.
Waves like the Appalachian ranges,
gray meeting gray,

boredom and torpedoes a heady mix, oh,
how do you keep them down on the farm
after they've seen Paree?

The topography of those ranges
the ropy muscles of my father's arms,
the taut veins on his temples
that looped across his balding head
to disappear somewhere
up there and seep down to dark:
what lay behind his eyes,
what caught his throat.

Time stumbles in the gnarled valleys
where anthracite and bitumen
elbow bones, and men
wore down their teeth
on hard wind and miner's wages,
and children stole away on slow flapping wings
like the odd heron on the flyway,
one eye on the Connemaugh,
one on the next ridge.

Blair, Huntingdon, Mifflin, Juniata,
leviathan ribs of mountain force the roads to follow.
No way but down,
or up the arc to Jersey.
Cambria, Somerset, Indiana, Clearfield:
roads circle back on themselves here.
No way for a sober man
to get to Nanty Glo.

On Hearing the Call to Prayer over the Marcellus Shale on Easter Morning

How like we are crinoids: Lily-like, nervous, as a starfish,
many fingered, prying crevice and fissure,
regrowing arms with every loss. A cry, a crying,
a call out, strange song, predawn trembling.
Through the permeable membrane, air

metes its punishment. An egg,
forgotten, now rotten, its inside resembling something
marbled. Things are seldom as hard as they seem.
I believe in *this*, called what you will;
and if a prayer can rise me breadlike,

so the day is risen. To walk (yea, though I walk)
a dry streambed, pick and pocket the sparkle of pyrite.
Small things have lain themselves here,
becoming in rock the fullness, then
the absence of themselves. A complex equation,

x contains multitudes, contradictions, can be
both positive or negative, influenced one day
by the preponderance of greater than
nothing; one day by weight of less than.
How can we solve ourselves, as zero is no answer, and x

resides always in the community of variables?
When everything is about to start, sleepless,
stumbling, stand to praise: Still nest. The hay
gleams as if lit. Emergent: a yellow chair, a red. The pond reach.
A swamp reveals the dead pine, the living moss,
even as the man's song ends.

Low Tide, Cobscook

You leave the waste of basin,
disheveled crab, one leg
severed and washed away.

Above a sheen of jasper,
I clothe myself
against your dearth
in weeds, in nacre.

GLASS FACTORY RUIN

Myself among the fallen
leaves, in a puddle I believe,
but such stillness.

I blink. I blink. Reach toward
me, a hard surface, silvered.
The pane, now busted, a confusion of inside

and out; 3,600 degrees Celsius
to transform sand to a substance that refracts.
Now this thicket of ashes, stone debris

a mirror of our own finity.
That we leave our artifacts
to shatter reflects, perhaps, as makers, our dilemma:

a-man-a-plan-a-canal-Panama,
the palindrome of things we've made
when we turn aside so ceaselessly unmade,

as I am a tel built of what I've found,
worn down by what I've forgotten.
But for what I've remembered,

what do I know of the world?
In here to make a vase or sheet, the teaser tweaked the fire,
a gaffer poked the glory

hole with a bolt; or spilled a pour:
a flowing marver. Light caught the checks and cords,
and the puntil was peeled of moil.

This eye captures light, flips it around.
This brain twists it upside down,
then sifts the light and shadow

against all I've known
to search for signs of hazard and make sense
of the confusion:

a doorless wall, a small arbor residing inside.
What I swore were some long-dead
worker's lunchtime toothpicks will

turn out to be a porcupine's quills.
The act of remembering is itself a conjure.
Molten glass spun out over a plane

is thickest at the courseway;
ripples are captured as it cools
so, with my moves,

the world in the windowpane
shifts, as if itself melting toward rain.
My odd job: to reconstruct

what's left behind, though it can cut.
Man-made myself, I'm on my knees
trying to find a little piece.

Implications of the Assumption

The average small bird
eats half its weight in insects and berries
so the day's attentions are
admirably focused, none of the
burden of recreation nor flying
desires, simply talon
to mouth. But sometimes cardinals
will dash through the backyard
as if nothing is at stake.

* * *

A hawk perched on the dead tree
picks away at the small bird
pinned under its claw,
its hooked beak unstuffing it,
so the trunk seems to be
shredding petals in fountain flume.

* * *

My pears are imports and broccoli is
year round. I buy cheese
from Denmark or a factory
in Wisconsin that oranges it up
and injects it into a can.
My shaving cream can smell like rain.

Many of my teeth
are fake. Some things are
too easily won.

* * *

Why won't the parakeet
swerve to miss the one
in the mirror? Like a pronghorn
it flies head first at the Other.
So is the self sometimes so

hard to meet that things shatter,
the room shards. Whatever
is gathered from the encounter
can wound quick on the flesh,
yield to what's sharp.

* * *

Blood surprises, startles,
the physical self suddenly
revealed as liquid.

* * *

These days cutting is all the rage
among the emotive adolescent set.
As if scars will tell them something

about themselves, or as if
they are the only world
on which they can make
their mark.

* * *

Are our minds as easily creased,
readily colored, shred?
Don't we know enough
not to reveal too much,
as the yellow-bibbed lorikeet
is ultimately the victim
of its own violent colors?

BELL

My friend Joan is uncomfortable with silence
so even crossing the street simultaneous with a stranger
ignites her to attempt to connect, fire some pleasantry
or little joke out across the breach that separates us all,

even as I now scrawl this every day to you,
although it will end up enfolded
in a notebook, and some school class scrolls simple notes
and ties them to helium balloons, or a castaway
speaks through the slender throat of a bottle,

and the Voyager spacecraft spins out
through the lace curtain
of our universe singing a song to the next.
We *must* say, urgent through a fine line quivering:
Come here, I want to see you.

Mid-January

Sun has Swissed the southern hill,
thaw has slawed the trails. It's lunch
time for the stirring flies.

The puddle in the drive is a sand tea
that tires sip and spit. I regret
I've squandered so much spirit

to idle hungers, so I ask you to dine,
prepare a pot of beef and turnip
and we'll drink an amber port

in the storm of warmth that's unsettled
me enough to be gentle again, to touch
your lips with my worn linen napkin.

Eden (an alternate version)

for Hailey

As if we had grown from the fallen plums,
the sun-hot and mudded, the bee deep buzz,

as if the table up from roots and we its wayward
branches, the cloth a smooth bark and glow,

and we as blossoms or, older now, as fruit, ripening
ruddy, our scent our singing,

the laughter our tree's come-hither
to what will allow us, wind and weather,

the eager hands, the blessing. For we are merry
vessels. We are ready. Ah yes, we are plenty.

DISTILLATION

On Albonini's "Adagio in G Minor"

Leaves lip wall,
wall arbor vitae,
treetop cloud,

cloud sky. Foxglove
grows not to please
but be sexed, release,

and die. The reseeding
a random fling,
beautiful in its inadvertence

and its insistence.
Night has come again.
A stillness as awful as full:

what could be called peace.
Quick tap:
rain on rhododendron.

I grow in silence,
its yawning. As if to start.

Equinox

you me muddle your elaborate what
rust wren rare in the quenched green
tinder winter wrap

hour hour hour hour

me you clutch founder until giving
you float me I float reflexive
and going come go come go

Time Series: Jordan River

"Definitively desacralized, time presents itself as
a precarious and evanescent duration, leading
irremediably to death."
— *Mircea Eliade*, The Sacred and the Profane

1.
A barbed wire spiraled,
flowing along a wall,

deft twist of ribbon,
a rose's thorns. We have begun

to mortify ourselves,
flesh as easy to shred as a petal.

Have we made time to crucify?
The fashion is forward, past written over, plangent.

The planet's pale glow, our water's rising.
We hold so hard we're sanctified.

2.
A carpet. A blanket. A shroud

wet with dew and heavy,

impressing the face, smudge of chin,

touches lips, the pressed nose,

forehead. Cellar smell of damp

stone and moldy rags, the last-flesh stench

of rotting mouse. Under the sheet edge

half a hand out of shadow, ovoid nails,

slight curve to the outer finger,

sharp lunge of wrist bone. The small scar.

My god, my god.

3.
       Constancy of flux, as of words
rising, its muscle a mesmer.
             All slight things fall to

from edge and sky, give,
       leap — gone. A reach;
             perhaps, take. This let-me-be-a-part.
       A mirrored, breath sucking
softness.
       Dimmable surge,
             sourcing from the creviced earth,
aged.
       Clouds become bound in roots,
             rethinking their form,
the roundness repeating
                dissipating,
                    breaking.

       Whipped and whited, the tick
tick of it rattles into a vast
       cup remeeting itself charged and risible.

       What cannot be held
         holds.

THE CURVE TRACED OUT FROM A POINT THAT MOVES SO ITS DISTANCE FROM THE POINT IS CONSTANT

A stinking carcass
scrawled on a rock
jeweled by departing

tide, a seal,
but mostly fish
fleshed and jabbed,

dropped or dragged,
swept up the beach,
or crabs unlimbed,

sometimes a seabird,
shrugging and squashed,
its feathers mopping tenderly

the tidal basin,
the dead
things wake me,

make me believe
in the poetry
of circle:

as swept we'll be
to the curling, restless sea,
so from its ooze we rise.

At Dusk

Purpose unceasing, for all its loopdiloo, the swallow
    is urgent —

surging: its sky riding: insects,
sex, and the nudge of young. Its shadow in the umber

river at evening simply an other. Do not mistake this
for yourself,   nor make of it

a metaphor for your own
spiraling desires. You are you are

on your own, not a feather
to your name.

But turning.
       Turning.

NOTES

"Remember me": "Remember me, but ah, forget my fate" are lyrics from Dido's lament from Purcell's opera *Dido and Aeneas.*

"On Hearing the Call to Prayer": "Yea, though I walk..." Psalm 23.

"Bell": "Come here, I want to see you" are the first words spoken over the telephone: Alexander Graham Bell to his assistant, Mr. Watson.

"Time Series": "My god my god..." Matthew 27:46.

About the Author

Marilyn McCabe's poem "On Hearing the Call to Prayer over the Marcellus Shale on Easter Morning" was awarded A Room of Her Own Foundation's 2012 Orlando Prize and appeared in the *Los Angeles Review*. Her first poetry collection, *Perpetual Motion*, was published by The Word Works in the Hilary Tham Capital Collection (2011). Her work has appeared in literary magazines such as *Nimrod*, *Valparaiso Poetry Review*, and *Painted Bride Quarterly*, her French translations and songs on *Numero Cinq*, and a video-poem on *The Continental Review*. She blogs about writing and reading at marilynonaroll.wordpress.com.

About the Artist

Victoria Palermo is a sculptor whose work is imbued with qualities of translucency, reflectivity, and the interplay of light and color. She resides in upstate New York.

About The Word Works

The Word Works, a nonprofit literary organization, publishes contemporary poetry and presents public programs. Imprints include the the Hilary Tham Capital Collection, The Washington Prize, International Editions, and The Tenth Gate Prize. A reading period is also held in May.

Monthly, The Word Works offers free literary programs in the Chevy Chase, MD, Café Muse series, and each summer, it holds free poetry programs in Washington, D.C.'s Rock Creek Park. Annually in June, two high school students debut in the Joaquin Miller Poetry Series as winners of the Jacklyn Potter Young Poets Competition. Since 1974, Word Works programs have included: "In the Shadow of the Capitol," a symposium and archival project on the African American intellectual community in segregated Washington, D.C.; the Gunston Arts Center Poetry Series; the Poet Editor panel discussions at The Writer's Center; and Master Class workshops.

As a 501(c)3 organization, The Word Works has received awards from the National Endowment for the Arts, the National Endowment for the Humanities, the D.C. Commission on the Arts & Humanities, the Witter Bynner Foundation, Poets & Writers, The Writer's Center, Bell Atlantic, the David G. Taft Foundation, and others, including many generous private patrons.

The Word Works has established an archive of artistic and administrative materials in the Washington Writing Archive housed in the George Washington University Gelman Library. It is a member of the Community of Literary Magazines and Presses and its books are distributed by Small Press Distribution.

wordworksbooks.org

OTHER WORD WORKS BOOKS

Karren L. Alenier, *Wandering on the Outside*
Karren L. Alenier, ed., *Whose Woods These Are*
Karren L. Alenier & Miles David Moore, eds.,
   Winners: A Retrospective of the Washington Prize
Christopher Bursk, ed., *Cool Fire*
Grace Cavalieri, *Creature Comforts*
Barbara Goldberg, *Berta Broadfoot and Pepin the Short*
Frannie Lindsay, *If Mercy*
Ayaz Pirani, *Happy You Are Here*
W.T. Pfefferle, *My Coolest Shirt*
Jacklyn Potter, Dwaine Rieves, Gary Stein, eds.,
   Cabin Fever: Poets at Joaquin Miller's Cabin
Robert Sargent, *Aspects of a Southern Story*
   & *A Woman from Memphis*
Nancy White, ed., *Word for Word*

INTERNATIONAL EDITIONS

Kajal Ahmad (Alana Marie Levinson-LaBrosse, Mewan
   Nahro Said Sofi, Darya Abdul-Karim Ali Najin, trans.,
   with Barbara Goldberg), *Handful of Salt*
Keyne Cheshire (trans.), *Murder at Jagged Rock: A*
   Tragedy by Sophocles
Yoko Danno & James C. Hopkins, *The Blue Door*
Moshe Dor, Barbara Goldberg, Giora Leshem, eds.,
   The Stones Remember: Native Israeli Poets
Moshe Dor (Barbara Goldberg, trans.), *Scorched by the Sun*
Lee Sang (Myong-Hee Kim, trans.), *Crow's Eye View:*
   The Infamy of Lee Sang, Korean Poet
Vladimir Levchev (Henry Taylor, trans.), *Black Book of*
   the Endangered Species

THE HILARY THAM CAPITAL COLLECTION

Mel Belin, *Flesh That Was Chrysalis*
Carrie Bennett, *The Land Is a Painted Thing*
Doris Brody, *Judging the Distance*
Sarah Browning, *Whiskey in the Garden of Eden*
Grace Cavalieri, *Pinecrest Rest Haven*
Cheryl Clarke, *By My Precise Haircut*
Christopher Conlon, *Gilbert and Garbo in Love*
    & *Mary Falls: Requiem for Mrs. Surratt*
Donna Denizé, *Broken like Job*
W. Perry Epes, *Nothing Happened*
Bernadette Geyer, *The Scabbard of Her Throat*
Barbara G. S. Hagerty, *Twinzilla*
James Hopkins, *Eight Pale Women*
Brandon Johnson, *Love's Skin*
Marilyn McCabe, *Perpetual Motion*
Judith McCombs, *The Habit of Fire*
James McEwen, *Snake Country*
Miles David Moore, *The Bears of Paris* & *Rollercoaster*
Kathi Morrison-Taylor, *By the Nest*
Tera Vale Ragan, *Reading the Ground*
Michael Shaffner, *The Good Opinion of Squirrels*
Maria Terrone, *The Bodies We Were Loaned*
Hilary Tham, *Bad Names for Women* & *Counting*
Barbara Louise Ungar, *Charlotte Brontë, You Ruined My Life*
    & *Immortal Medusa*
Jonathan Vaile, *Blue Cowboy*
Rosemary Winslow, *Green Bodies*
Michele Wolf, *Immersion*
Joe Zealberg, *Covalence*

THE TENTH GATE PRIZE

Jennifer Barber, *Works on Paper*, 2016
Lisa Sewell, *Impossible Object*, 2015

THE WASHINGTON PRIZE

Nathalie F. Anderson, *Following Fred Astaire*, 1998

Michael Atkinson, *One Hundred Children Waiting for a Train*, 2001

Molly Bashaw, *The Whole Field Still Moving Inside It*, 2013

Carrie Bennett, *biography of water*, 2004

Peter Blair, *Last Heat*, 1999

John Bradley, *Love-in-Idleness: The Poetry of Roberto Zingarello*, 1995, 2nd edition 2014

Christopher Bursk, *The Way Water Rubs Stone*, 1988

Richard Carr, *Ace*, 2008

Jamison Crabtree, *Rel[AM]ent*, 2014

Barbara Duffey, *Simple Machines*, 2015

B. K. Fischer, *St. Rage's Vault*, 2012

Linda Lee Harper, *Toward Desire*, 1995

Ann Rae Jonas, *A Diamond Is Hard But Not Tough*, 1997

Frannie Lindsay, *Mayweed*, 2009

Richard Lyons, *Fleur Carnivore*, 2005

Elaine Magarrell, *Blameless Lives*, 1991

Fred Marchant, *Tipping Point*, 1993, 2nd edition 2013

Ron Mohring, *Survivable World*, 2003

Barbara Moore, *Farewell to the Body*, 1990

Brad Richard, *Motion Studies*, 2010

Jay Rogoff, *The Cutoff*, 1994

Prartho Sereno, *Call from Paris*, 2007, 2nd edition 2013

Enid Shomer, *Stalking the Florida Panther*, 1987

John Surowiecki, *The Hat City After Men Stopped Wearing Hats*, 2006

Miles Waggener, *Phoenix Suites*, 2002

Charlotte Warren, *Gandhi's Lap*, 2000

Mike White, *How to Make a Bird with Two Hands*, 2011

Nancy White, *Sun, Moon, Salt*, 1992, 2nd edition 2010

George Young, *Spinoza's Mouse*, 1996

www.ingramcontent.com/pod-product-compliance
Lightning Source LLC
Chambersburg PA
CBHW031006090426
42737CB00008B/697